D0056006

NEITHER WORLD

Winner of the 1995 James Laughlin Award
of The Academy of American Poets.

The James Laughlin Award supports
the publication of a poet's second book.
Originally known as the Lamont Poetry Selection,
it is now named in honor of the poet and publisher
James Laughlin, who founded New Directions in 1936.
The award is endowed by a gift to The Academy of
American Poets from the Drue Heinz Trust.

Judges for 1995:
Richard Kenney, David St. John, Heather McHugh

 The Ohio Arts Council helped fund
this organization with state tax dollars
to encourage economic growth,
educational excellence and cultural
enrichment for all Ohioans.

The Miami University Press Poetry Series
General Editor: James Reiss

NEITHER WORLD

Poems
by

Ralph Angel

Miami University Press
Oxford, Ohio

Library of Congress Cataloging-in-Publication Data

Angel, Ralph, 1951-
    Neither world : poems / by Ralph Angel.
        p. cm.
    ISBN 1-881163-12-1 : $15.95 – ISBN 1-881163-13-X : $9.95
    I. Title.
    PS3551.N457N45 1995   95-1768
    811'.54 – dc20   CIP

The paper in this book meets the guidelines
for permanence and durability of the Committee
on Production Guidelines for Book Longevity
of the Council on Library Resources. ∞

Printed in the U.S.A.

9 8 7 6 5 4 3 2 1

For my parents,
and my sisters Joanne and Vicki

Acknowledgments

Acknowledgment is made to the following publications for poems which originally appeared in them:

The American Poetry Review: "At Your Convenience," "Breaking and Entering," "Don't," "Evolving Similarities," "Love's That Simple," "The Blessed," "The Privilege of Silence," "Trance Music" and "Veils of Prayer"

The Antioch Review: "Breaking Rhythm," "Getting Honest," "Inside a World the World Fits Into," "It Could Have Been More," "Untitled" and "Where All the Streets Lead to the Sea"

Cimarron Review: "A Rat in the Room," "Like Land Crabs," "The River Has No Hair to Hold Onto" and "Try and Run"

College English: "Headlights Trail Away," "Subliminal Birds" and "Unspeakable"

Crazyhorse: "At the Seams," "From Goya's Room" and "Leaving One"

Indiana Review: "How Long Can We Go On Winning?"

The Missouri Review: "Long Shadows, Many Footsteps" and "Waves"

Passages North: "Among Fields of Shocked Corn"

Poetry: "And the Grass Did Grow," "In Every Direction," "Shadow Play" and "The Loneliest Man"

"Shadow Play" also appeared in *The Best American Poetry of 1988*

"Breaking and Entering," "Shadow Play" and "The River Has No Hair to Hold Onto" also appeared in *New American Poets of the '90s*

"It Could Have Been More" also appeared in *Forgotten Language: Contemporary Poets and Nature*

"Breaking Rhythm" also appeared in *Grand Passion: The Poets of Los Angeles and Beyond*

"And the Grass Did Grow," "Shadow Play" and "The Loneliest Man" were awarded *Poetry* magazine's Bess Hokin Prize

Contents

NEITHER WORLD

Long Shadows, Many Footsteps

And so, another cover bursts into flames.
And so, even nakedness
is only a symbol of doors opening.

This isn't a city, but a forest.
And a child on an adventure who
happens by a stone farmhouse

(and is offered warm milk there)
thinks he'll return again
and bring his friends–how happy they'll be–

even as an hour later
he's running freakishly through night's
black leaves, lost, trying to fetch his dog.

And there are grown-ups
with somewhere to go
who just keep on walking;

they remember later the white sink,
the bathtub, in a fire-gutted tenement.
For people, other people

can't be enough. These aren't
the faces of friends, but faint, disturbing
webs of alliance, long-winded stories

that we listen to desperately
but can't understand. The woman
who comes to me thinks that making

love can break a person down
and get to what he knows, but there's
nothing really to show her.

And in the dream that recurs each night
the apartment door opens to the blue
of a blue sky, and Hanula isn't there,

isn't visible, but here, the way
the sound of sod on the blessed's cold wood
is here. I don't know, I can't imagine,

I don't know about death,
but am learning to bury my own kind.

Subliminal Birds

Like the infant, wriggling free, tasting air,
hollering from the blue cliffs of Echo Park.

Like clear wind, like ashes rising from the tips of leaves,
or wooden storefronts in the must of towering construction.
And all that occurs while waiting, or forgetting,
the sound of a train in the heart's distance.

All that coming and going, so much
life spreading its wings in both worlds,
soaring beneath the crust of the handshake and signature,
between the lines of stories we tell
in order to be heard here,
in order to feel confidently at home.

Right here, where walls of survival are windows.
A whole galaxy of stars in the nod of the proprietor
of a carnival shooting gallery.
Where, ecstatically, with the blinds drawn,
a woman tumbles from her bed
into the swirling green waters of an Oriental carpet.

Where children, school kids

in grey and white uniforms, twirl
until the buildings
are dust on the parched lips of a storm,
a shimmering ribbon,
an indelible, radiant, haze.

Unspeakable

Summer has its way
around here. People kind of
cave in, weary
with the certainty of nighttime,
how it draws even these last
illusory shimmers of tropical ice
into its own oblivion.

And all the flowers
have withered away. The animals
too, are forgotten.
Now the pavement
keeps getting hotter.
City lights churn.
And out in those parking lots
and behind iron doors
your neighbors stare into their
billion broken mirrors.

A desire
perhaps to blame them,
to give them all new faces,
the ones you've painlessly

selected–brisk and cheerful–
until each prisoner's
freed from his imagined
demands, and all your hope
becomes your nature, out
among the lush foliage
of the future.

A desire to be noticed
perhaps, by the old guy
who rants in the stupid
glow of his icebox,
to show your scars
to the scowling landlady,
absolutely terrified
of lifting the lid of the dumpster,

to point them out,
to brush them aside with a laugh
and a wave of the hand
for the boy who
wanders these rooftops
each night, envying everyone

who can walk well enough
on the ground, even though
they're obvious and ordinary,

even though
what you'll finally speak of
does not belong to,
and no longer resembles,
your wound.

The River Has No Hair to Hold Onto

It's only common sense (not that they know the score,
they don't avoid it). And so one's life story
is begun on a paper napkin and folded into a coat pocket
to be retrieved later when it's darker
and cooler, and closer. And onward

to rockier ground, where conversation is impassable
and human beings matter more than
the light that glimmers beneath the horizon
before sinking into our own inaudible sigh (a long way
from these fur-covered hands). And somehow

the deal is struck. Money gets made.
And the small shocks one undergoes for no reason,
the bus driver handing you a transfer, a steamy
saxophone ascending the jungle. The city
lays down its blanket of rippling

lamplight as though exhaustion too
was achieved by consensus, and what one does
and how one feels have nothing to do with one's self.
No, this can't be the place, but it must be
the road that leads there, always beginning

when morning is slow and hazy, suffering to
    get somewhere
with all the memorable mistakes along the way,
piecing them together, arriving,
believing that one arrives at a point different from
the starting point, admitting things still aren't clear.

A rag doll on a dark lawn injures the heart
as deeply as the salt sea air filling one's lungs
with the sadness once felt in a classroom,
a sadness older than any of us.
And the dogs barking, challenging cars. And the willows

lining the sidewalk, lifting their veils
to the inscrutable surface of wood. (Someone
is trying to get a message through. Someone thinks
you'll understand it).

The Privilege of Silence

No threats. Not the teaser
this time. Finally there is a random God.
And all the filthy laundry we've hung out to dry,
all the fingers we've grown used to pointing,
sneer, backbite, everything that worked
yesterday, nothing a little
breeze won't knock down.

Even wisdom, the pure heart, the woman
who for six days among impatient nurses
choked on water, who knew a full
life when she saw one, who never asked of anybody,
begged for air, was made
to beg for something
she knew she was en route to.

Only the living take things for granted.
The dead don't leave; some part of us
is missing. And we sense
the echo, the wind in our
veins, faces like thin
curtains that let in the light
and let loose our shadows.

Even asleep, in the ancient dance,
we are turning away.
Turning toward the ruckus
of jacarandas. A face in the crowd
that offers itself like early morning,
unknowingly, as we are drawn to it.
More strangely than that.

Waves

Sweeping through the branches
of leaves, old sensations
dampening collars, tugging at sleeves . . .
With our boots on a curbside, our faces, the clouds,
the past at least is faithful—never
to be worked out right, never undone.

And we might remember ourselves
someday, pulling close
our overcoats, a fine freeze of breath
trailing away. We *were* nervous, as though
moving forward would merely uncover
the time it takes to be here.

Murmur of traffic.
A foghorn crawling across the bay . . .
What is left behind spreads thinly,
overlapping. And perhaps the shattered bottle
gives us back, or the horizon's
implosion, close and

amorphous as a feeling that spans years,
lifetimes, the cities of solitary ocean.
And our language is clearly alien,
dressed funny, gathered each day
around some table in a public park
where refugees shuffle the cards

and drink tea. Where we
chat prices and weather and flesh,
argue the winnings, the lousy
luck of the losers, until we arrive at
the last things we might say, calling home
the unseen, and setting it free.

The Loneliest Man

You're serious, aren't you.
And everyone you've ever bumped into
understands and graciously bows out of sight.

Down on the avenue the world
is clearly outlined. There's nothing there,
or each thing seems fixed in place
so not to disturb whoever it is
you think you are just now.

You've so much to fall back on.
"The way the game is played" and "only
a matter of time." Dots on the map
like sentries, like ciphers, the many rooms and
houses of memory that make an afternoon familiar,
vandalizing breath,
draining the colors of friends and passers-by
until the space between them vanishes.

You drop in, you do lunch,
and it feels just horrible
to want to help you, convince you
of how miserable you are, not nearly

close enough, and never far enough away
from the rest of us,

the less fortunate, breaking down
in the thick of it, complaining again
or calling it even–
on the front stoop, on the jagged hilltop,
watching a thin sky as it darkens on our eyes:

pinpricks of light
opening up a universe without end.

Leaving One

I don't want any numbers.
I'm worn out beforehand.
I don't care about
who's sleeping with whom.
I only know what people don't tell me,
how it's difficult to be a human being,
that the complication begins inside
the way loneliness can't be
located in any one part of the body,
that it rises from the surface
where the soul should be
and rears its ugly head
in the face of anything tender,
those fingers of yours, those knees.

You sit beside me at the window.
We are not drinking the coffee,
we don't eat the toast.
Outside, in the park, two huge maples
are ablaze with Indian summer,
and absolutely still.
People parade the sidewalks,

brush against one another at crossings.
No one needs to understand anything
to get the goods on everyone.
It's the way of morning,
a malicious, well-trained avoidance.

My staying here
would not protect you, these fingers
of yours, the soul in your shy eyes,
I'd simply go down trying.
We, right here, belong to us.
But I'm calling the shots now,
and now I'm leaving this hotel.
With all we've lost already
our pores are wide open.
And it's cold out there.
Come drive with me.

How Long Can We Go On Winning?

We can still walk away from what we don't believe in
the way fathers hide their lives
when power slips like rings from their
fingers. And their children come to taunt them,
needing so much to remain shadows.

No. Nothing. Nobody saves us.
Not the job, or its salary, or its house and car.
Not the friend who complains, and cries,
and comforts.

Admit it. We've let each other down. And then,
congratulations. We knew exactly what would happen.
The canvas shoes and warm Cokes.
Those great, dull buildings
and the mad twilight–
alone at last! Where it's easy to reveal nothing,
and no one depends on our wanting to be known.

In Every Direction

As if you had actually died in that dream
and woke up dead. Shadows of untangling vines
tumble toward the ceiling. A delicate
lizard sits on your shoulder, its eyes
blinking in every direction.

And when you lean forward and present your
hands to the basin of water, and glimpse the glass face
that is reflected there, it seems perfectly at home
beneath the surface, about as unnatural
as nature forcing everyone to face the music
with so much left to do, with everything
that could be done better tomorrow, to dance
the slow shuffle of decay.

Only one season becoming another,
continents traveling the skyway, the grass
breathing. And townspeople, victims, murderers,
the gold-colored straw and barbed-wire hair of
    the world
wafting over the furrows, the slashed roads
to the door of your office or into the living room.

The towel is warm and cool, soft to the touch,
but in another dream altogether
a screen door creaks open, slams shut,
and across the valley a car's headlights swing up
and over. And maybe you are the driver
with both hands on the wheel, humming a tune
nobody's ever heard before,

or maybe the woman on the edge of the porch,
grown quiet from fleeing,
tough as nails.

Breaking and Entering

Many setups. At least as many falls.
Winter is paralyzing the country, but not here.
Here, the boys are impersonating songs of indigenous
wildlife. Mockingbird on the roof of the Gun Shop,
scrub jay behind the Clear Lake Saloon.
And when she darts into a drugstore for a
    chocolate-covered
almond bar, sparrow hawks get the picture
and drive off in her car.

Easy as 8th & Spring Street,
a five-course meal the size of a dime.
Easy as vistas admired only from great distance,
explain away the mystery
and another thatched village is cluster-bombed.
Everyone gets what he wants nowadays.
Anything you can think of is probably true.

And so, nothing. Heaven on earth. The ruse
of answers. A couple-three-times around the block
and ignorance is no longer a good excuse.
There were none. Only moods

arranged like magazines and bones, a Coke bottle
full of roses, the dark, rickety tables about the room.
And whenever it happens, well, it's whatever it takes,
a personality that is not who you are
but a system of habitual reactions to another
light turning green, the free flow of
traffic at the center of the universe where shops
are always open and it's a complete
surprise each time you're told that minding
    your own business
has betrayed your best friend. But that's over,
that's history, the kind of story that tends to have an ending,
the code inside your haunted head.

Easy as guilt. As waking and sleeping, sitting down
to stand up, sitting down to go out walking,
closing our eyes to see in the nocturnal
light of day. "Treblinka
was a primitive but proficient
production line of death," says a former
    SS Unterscharfürer
to the black sharecropper-grandchild of slavery

who may never get over
the banality of where we look.

Only two people
survived the Warsaw uprising, and the one
whose eyes are paths inward, down into the soft grass,
into his skeleton,
who chain-smokes and drinks, is camera shy,
wears short-sleeved shirts, manages to mumble,
"If you could lick my heart, it would poison you."

At the Seams

When I think I see clearly and, therefore, think
    about thinking about,
let me be in the dark, measure and strain, let this old
bread stand for sustenance, I may choose not to eat it.
And when I think it's okay to sleep
or that memory's a comfort less malicious than
happiness, give me the courage
to deal these cards to the wind
and keep walking.

All day long the world sings to itself.
Buildings don't change color, don't
shimmy, they don't lie. But two people in the
    same room,
the one with a lump in her throat, the other changing
the channel, the five
billion lives that hang on their going through with it,
just like that, busting up some ceiling.

In the damp garden of faces our eyes
twitch like shooting stars, a stitch of
bone. Ghost vein, hinterland, echo-of-eternity,
    it takes

practice to get lost, paint with our own hair,
    burrow deeply
into shadows of flesh coming undone at the seams.
Over billowing grasses, fierce grasses,
a low branch settles for a handful of splinters.
Take more.
Take more than you can repay.

Veils of Prayer

When the sky darkens
and turns white, and the green
and blue leaves deepen–
showers of mist, bamboo, the lemons shine.
A light was left on, white azalea, I had left a light
    on for you.
Do not come back, not now. Though still here
I too can't return.

Only the edges
go on like this, long into dusk, the soul
drains us in seconds.
And the nothing that's left, and the no more
hope, and what I wouldn't
kill off or trade away, fuck over, dismiss, make a
    joke of, this
failure of solitude, my own dark
standing alone in the dark hand that feeds me.

Into this night . . . and drunker.
The drone of the crickets. Voices without mouths,
    without glare,
the fence just fading away, everything

and my own exhausted space,
to privacy.
                    Into this night,
I swear it, years disappear without a voice of your own,
a middle ground, all those
reasons for giving in, for holding on, leaving

again and again,
to poison—all those islands of blame.
                              And ain't nobody lives there.
Trees high on the ridge. The laconic wires.
Lit windows and shutting down.
A sigh in the shrubs, on the porches, and shutting down.
When the sky darkens . . .
When the dark finds the needle . . .

Please. Not ever.
I'm still failing. Unforgiven. Alone.
That you can be right if you want to.
I won't recognize you.
That we may never be resolved.
That I may be at peace.
That I may heal into the husk of my heart.

Evolving Similarities

I know there are pigeons smaller than we are
roaming the parks and the alleys.
I have seen us go down lightly
and sideways
and get back home again one day at a time.
For people like us
there are pigeons everywhere.

I know moss-covered brick
and the short walk back to the studio.
I'm familiar with reclining nudes
and the orange goldfish.
In the dankest of circumstances
I too have dialed the number
and thought twice and tested each one of them

as if anybody stands a chance around here
and no one carries our messages.
If there's something you still need
believe me

they will pick up the phone.

Because the body's *not* stupid.
Because the flesh remembers
and taking care comes first.
A young mother cradles an infant to her breast
and it feels like love.
Like we can do something.

Because you would save every last one of them
you are already forgiven.
It doesn't matter now
that nothing in this world is direct.
Our life is layered.
First we weep
and then we listen and eat something
and weep again

and listen.
And eat again.
And it doesn't matter anymore
at the bottom of your story

at the very-most bottom of recovery.
And confession.
And then popped for it.
Even the one who's picked up unconscious
is resisting arrest.

And it just happens to be perfectly okay
to feel like you're understood.
They'll follow you anywhere.
They will peck at your shoes in the plaza.
A cluster of violets on the floor of the rain forest
pumping water

making food.

I know that dread is wrapped up in knowing.
I know the way dread tends to consume itself.
And I apologize
for just barely listening.
But if I cry tonight
tell me
who is there among us who will call your bluff?

Love's That Simple

At those who love you, who look up to you or just
    happen to feel like human beings
because of you. Even the moon would shed its skin,
the infant its shadow for you.

I mean you can if you want to,
in the face of, at whatever it is you think you can buy.
Money itself, or childhood, or somewhere to run to,
    someone impatient enough to speak for you.
You're no fool, you're entitled. And the only way
to avoid pain is to inflict it on somebody else.

But you *haven't* disappeared them,
though they're there for you. In gardens of sulfur,
    with blackened walls, until the heart is tamed and
    my lips bleed.
And intimacy, a taunt. And trust,
a stratagem. Your mama's racism.
Your daddy's legalese.

Here are the spiders that will crawl through your eyes.
Passion. Resilience. The wild, cold colors
of the Mediterranean. What if all you can do is despise

what you came for? The flawless. The seamless.
You've invented everyone!

Talk to them. What they think about and feel.
What they'll do the next time.
You, who are not responsible, chased by nothing, who
    limp nowhere. Tell them
about the mountain and the kingdom within.

And resentment. Betrayal. You had such high hopes
    for them.
The no one who takes a back seat to you,
who won't live up to whatever it was,
it's just too complicated.

We either forgive one another who we really are
or not.

At Your Convenience

Whether it blew up in your face
or on television. From the driver's seat, into just about
any household. Most of the sink is there,
and the plumbing beneath it.
The cabinet.
Part of a wall.

Whatever sold the paper, kicked ass,
Thank God, in the courtroom. Where it's
hidden in a hospice, an old folks home, as if you've
done yourself a favor this time.
Not even children breathe around here.

Into what language does the raised voice disappear?
Which alphabet will throw open
the shutters, add on a couple of more rooms,
Thank God, and pee in the roses, lose its footing
and go on dancing?

Tonight, the neighbors are breaking up furniture.
They are breaking bottles and kicking cans

and circling the block.
Tonight, the neighbors scream into plastic bags,
so maybe you're right, nobody's
yelling at you.

And so what? Even thinking about it
is an example of tears–as if the question in the
    air tonight
is How do I deal with this problem?–
already crystallized, faked out by experience,
perfected, adorned.

In front of everyone. Deep down,
and rid of.
Not that you don't know what they're saying.
You do. You know what they're talking about.
Not that there ever was a problem.
It's just that you disagree.

Trance Music

And even less.
The bottom-most stairs.
A door like that, wide open.
The last bright-grey, shady traces–
as a cloud of starlings
rising up from nowhere, floating off
to nowhere.

For the shape of.
The view! The terrible scream
as it comes to an end. In hair grown thick
and long. Into his bewilderment.
The eyes of her self-portrait,
without blinking!

That in its
very shudder. From the trampled grass
that springs back, and the drowned
face rising to the surface of stone.
From dressed in rags,

this was the house,

and the bones show through.
And less than that. Under other moons,
in another breeze. For the first time.

Headlights Trail Away

and go on surprising. It happens.
Everything. A couple of suitcases
falling from a fourth-story apartment–
fertilize the African violets
and there you have it, new slippers
in the hallway–the relentless, invisible
moon of my heart, hugging its orbit.

Yes, it's raining,
or about to. Black splotches
on the sidewalk. Gum wrappers
in a gutter stream. I feel I've
changed so many times in the last
fifteen seconds that the cold
must belong to the fishwoman's
darker eye, sparrows in the hollow
of a traffic light.

All else is habit, like believing
you're right, you're a decent, good person.
It's the same street, no matter
what punches are thrown, the same
signs. A house of cards

with a barber stropping the razor
and the janitor jangling keys,
with packages to wrap, the several breezes.
There is the faintest trace of basil
on the breath of the waitress.
It tickles, that taste,
and what can you do?
Such a pleasure to be here.

Among Fields of Shocked Corn

And what about what the slow
undulation of farmland
is doing to the sky?
There is one quiet cloud there
keeping the world at bay,
tearing itself apart.

Sugar maples. Red oaks.
The hardwoods are the most
fragile, a shivering beauty,
the long fall to dirt heaven.
I know now how a farmhouse
was the invention of distance.
The hay is rolled, the silos
gleam as if there's
something left worth saving.

And the old farmer
on his tractor, plowing
salt into the furrows
so that a man might never get up,
stand on his good two feet,
sleep with his wife and

walk away again.
I own less and less
of myself. I rented

this sucker to get out of town,
and now I want to drive up
onto that median and
turn it around. I have one last
favor to ask of just about
everyone: whatever you do,
don't confuse Ralph Angel
with Ralph Angel. Today,
he loves everything too much.

And I want it simple,
a small breath filling the world
with tremendous music.
Among fields of shocked corn
you are stepping into your car.
Stranger, my love, you really are.
Place your hands on my chest.
You can trust me.
See, they go right through.

Like Land Crabs

skittering sideways
when the moon drives by, the blank stare
of the boulevard, and everyone carrying something.

Eating a double-dog chili burrito
seems like a perfectly natural thing to do.
Nothing much matters because
so much turns into a face

that looks back at you. Blundering,
I think. It's out of the question, the night.
Out of the hands at the ends of my arms
on the hips of the lush who's undressing me.

Everyone keeps getting in
and out of cars. I'm electrified
by earth shoes, a solitary goat dance,
the weird expanse of parking lots,
glittering, peopled with loneliness.

Past news racks and policemen, past
all-night doctors carving up corners
in bedsheets of torn light, I follow a friend

who swears I know where I'm going
among headless palm trees
and other fences.

"Bring on the coffee," I hear myself
say as you reach over and turn on
the radio, "I didn't know I was already driving."
I brake for a stop sign.
The earth speeds up a little.

A Rat in the Room

What a guy goes through these days
to get his uncle Leo to pass him a couple of lentils!
Every twisted crime of the century. All manner of jugular
and spit. "You're a loser, kid."

Then the sun goes down. A fork
whizzes by. How could I have imagined it,
my hands around his throat, this jumping up and down?
I thought that might make us closer. Everything
    out on the table,
enough to drive you crazy, a guy could
kill someone!–until a vase of snapdragons is knocked over

and the pot roast lands on cousin Regina,
until, finally, the cauliflower, the brussels sprouts
are ridiculous, the way the truth can be ridiculous
whenever it's finally found.

And that's it. The worst
and best times. Billboards and lightning,
black trees in a rearview mirror
and out of this life. Another five minutes alone
and I won't be able to keep myself company,

like a security guard patrolling
expensive homes, taking from them the framed
and pampered objects, not just to get himself busted
but because having been caught will make him
    more interesting.

Some part of me downs a stiff one
and knows too well his miserable moment of euphoria.
And a side I've had some luck in hiding
rifles the medicine cabinet before losing consciousness.
Sometimes, you have to be a totally different person
looking over his shoulder, back at you,
in order to see what it is you're up to.

An insomniac's light
flicks on in a neighbor's apartment, and old-man Riley
paces his living room. He smokes
a Marlboro. And another.
He punches the channel selector of his remote control.
With a scalpel, a disgruntled alien
is stabbing a patient. Riley jacks up the volume.
First the legs, then the face, the breast,
the back of the neck. And one by one,

everybody in the building is awake.
The creaking floorboards. Small
shudders in the plaster. Miss Julie, the hairdresser,
sprawls over a chair, sharpening nails.
Aroma of reheated coffee.
The Murphys think they're hungry, grease the skillet
for a tall stack of sweet-and-sour flapjacks.
And the ancient, most honorable, Mrs. Costello
pokes her head out a ground-floor
bedroom window, looking tired
and skyward. "Is somebody gonna do me a favor
and shut that nut up?"

Old-man Riley, he can't sleep.
It's what he wanted.

Try and Run

Okay, all right, I was itching for a little
relaxation.
Nobody plans the explosions these days.
Not the disciples of pavement,
not those *other* guys.
The street's a lake, a fire, a mirror,
but I'd like to know what's
poking out at the skin.

So maybe I'm hungry.
And maybe the trouble with all these cafeterias
is they have so much damn food around.
I mean too much of anything, I mean
you know what I mean–spoonful
of grapefruit juice and I'm out of here.
It's going to come anyway.
And, probably, somebody's
going to live through it.

There we go.
The sirens. The pigeons.
The flowerpots. The air.
Between the collies and the pomeranians,

bitter feuding.
And the line at the DMV
is the line at the Vermont Ave. P.O.,
and the cabby throws the old fart
right out of his car, and listen, pal, there ain't
no way a cashier like her
needs your kind of aggravation.

Go ahead. Say something.
It'll be cruel.
But if a certain part of the brain arrives
it'll think it's figured everything out again—
a time to walk away from the table,
the dice were never not loaded.
I mean if a certain part of the brain
arrives, if a particularly
shitty part of the brain ever does get here,
my God, I've already become it.

Inside a World the World Fits Into

The lit match! As if I could really
see just now. The long streets, and longer river,
skyscrapers, and the arched bridges, all
that dusk has darkened,
all the distance they're related to.

And his voice is a sound gone wrong, a noisily
flapping one-winged bird. If not *clean,*
which word? His low, his spiraling, the heave and
thud of cold freight derailing, if not
orderly, what defends him from the truth
he already stands accused of?

As if, really, we'd been seen. In shaded areas,
in the hard, glazed open, standing in circles, laughing
at the worst possible time.

Breaking Rhythm

And then the head is at odds with the body.

And then the head strangles your way of thinking.

But don't get me wrong. It's not
that I'm saying life's taking us nowhere,

if I'm not saying *yes*, I'm a liar, a liar who does not
dwell in the shadow of his own home–

kind of your average, respectable, two-bit junkie
    who thinks he knows what he's after,
and what he's after is nightmare. Concussive. Brutal.
    The unending
ritual of eluding detection rising up and taking
shape with flaring nostrils and enormous hands,

and if it just happens to be pain that he's in right now,
well, at least, pain is who he is for a while.

No big deal. Out loud

the pulse quickens and, very loudly, prolongs itself.

Anger slams the door on a mettlesome friend of a friend,

and then I am boredom paying for groceries,
most happy when you chew on my chin
in luxurious sweat, in our sexual oil,

exhaustion on the subway back to the city. The fact is
I can only hear one part of myself at a time.

And it's late. And I'm tired. And it sounds like
all or nothing. A fistful of thirst and a cup of hot tea,

the silence shame gathers into no boundary.

The robe. The pocketknife. The loaves of bread.
Mud on the carpets. The shatter of leaves.

The wonder, the wonder, the wonder.

It Could Have Been More

In the sky above the clouds
nothing is falling. Lift and curl,
the wave's translucence. The pure blue sky
in the windows of bones,

by accident
the fold of the body, new skin for the wound.

And the clouds themselves, loose
and swept along. And the untouched rain
blowing through the empty rooms.
Was the need not always
for love, each loss

the same self breaking the heavens
into birds, birds into dark-massed trees?
I can't touch my own soul

though I know that I've dreamed it.
In a dream there are clothes, islands of
hair, snowdrifts flaring.

Boy child, dirty-faced and hopeful.
The woman who wakes up angry, overflowing,
grieving. Only one taste

in my mouth on the shoreline of brightness
and sky. Only one
and the feelings I've drowned!

Untitled

Surely everyone is born unfinished,
could use a great deal of life today, and dies enough,
enough to keep the wound from healing.

And a cry comes close. A siren
cuts across it. It's the dying that torments us,
taking something and in a hurry

as if it were a beauty that one couldn't bear,
taking something more. Surely everyone
suffers to the knees of the heart

when the heart is open.
And I don't recover. A cry
cuts across it. The red camellias cut across it

where rain drips from the eaves,
drums the stepping stones after a storm has
cleared the face of everything: porches

and cancer, pine trees, the bird on the white wing.
And the neighborhood blind dog. Little dwarf,
half hairless, half lame, punishes

the curb, the treacherous ivy. Our little
neighborhood comedian. Choke chain, chest puffed out,
yaps at the air, yapping the length of ultimate

driveways, sideways, backwards, until
another dog barks back. Look out! Each step
a shock of joy.

Where All the Streets Lead to the Sea

Where all the streets lead to the sea, and full-throated
canaries are free in their cages, and geraniums
splash deeply the shadows of buildings,
in those tiny, dark cages, a woman is singing from
    her balcony.

With her eyes closed, her voice is a prayer an old
widow is mouthing on the steps of the shuttered
cathedral, syllable by syllable, to the knot
    in her beads.

In that very pocket, every pocket, where the alleys,
where a man falls into himself and rises up and
    knows from the inside
the unbearable weight of a white suit,
the black boot polish in his hair threading slowly
    his cheek.

Whatever got scared
really is scared, that same child who
won't go to sleep because she can't comprehend how
    it might not

pull her under. Without her. Lost track of.
The one who coughs and with his hands pushes the
    air away
and coughs again. Those who bring sticks, pieces of
    broken-down
furniture, a door for the huge, flowering bonfires.

The thousands, walking. More or less sad. More or less
unaccommodated. The woman who in her
    granddaughter
scrunching her nose like that, tilting her head that way,

discovers again her own mother. And those two,
who got close, with their clothes on fire, it's *their*
    laughter
crashing onto the damp sand,
roaring.

From Goya's Room

Is it light
that defies knowledge and seeps out of the ground,
a ground that can never be seen?
A darkness that crowds, forcibly, all
that is human? At what miracle
is the blind beggar gazing? To what palpable
color in the freakishly realistic faces of awkward,
    vulnerable,
ordinary people? The violet white
of the water seller? The knife grinder's good, brown eye?
What is soft, and secret, and alive,
alone in the stairwells of smoke, with everybody
pressed together, alone in the innocence of the taverns?
Shy, rose-colored anemones? Murmuring stone?
Is it the ghostly imagination, floating figures
with the figures of blood raging below? A naked man
devouring the head of his son? The smeared
clown-faces of the aged, the carved masks
people grow into, transparent to radiance?
Will I never be able to tell you,
plainly, I no longer want to understand you?
That I just want to be with you?

Getting Honest

What goes down in the course of a day
means nothing to me, it means
nothing to me.
It's everything in the world to me.

One minute I'm on my way back to the city
and I hear myself say
that I'm not going to let it bother me. And I don't,
and it's over–wholly arbitrary.
I could have let it destroy me.
At any other moment I probably would have.

Right now he's thinking about all and anything.
It's a way of avoiding everything. "Don't worry,"
    he says,
"I knew you were lying."
And maybe I was. Out there
it goes badly for me.

And the Grass Did Grow

Nothing is happening,
and yet what is being acted out
or proven right now, flamboyantly,
might just turn a corner
and become the real thing.

Mostly holed up in a room
somewhere, or pacing the twilit
underworld of the neighborhood,
another honest display of emotion taking up
its fair share of available space,
and all the desire I can possibly
imagine, like a stone flung,
inscribing its arc of air.

But living is fickle, open-ended,
even the little myths break down.
Nobody thinks I'm very funny.
In fact, they're insulted.
They've exacted their portions
and now appear rather chipper,
scattering me over the hillsides

and into the night.
Like a pedestrian in a crosswalk
replaced by another man, I go with them.
And I don't go. The need remains
forever: to have, to get my hands on,
or to be taken, to lose myself
in a warmer, less urgent caress.

I open one eye, take a look around.
No pat answers, no permanence or rest.
Someone just happens to keep beginning,
and my life too, where I left it,
over there.

Don't

Even your reflexes will turn
brittle with too much anger, so much grief.

And the kingfisher that once
swooped over the river's rushing heartbeat

will come back a childish dream
that puts you down, carefully, to sleep.

Then, if it's written in a silhouette of trees,
in the dark of a pickup truck,

your own noise
will grow a little louder than the city,

and the inevitable sigh, from the very
depth of your earth, will sing

in the cracks, in the clear water
of everyone you are refusing to cling to.

And you will no longer hear those
who leave town and stay,

or the ones who return a few minutes later
as somebody else. Then, my friend,

this is not a personal story.
Please. Only then.

The Blessed

There is a place, I swear it,
where sadness fits, but with all this blood on our hands
we choose what to do and make ourselves up.

Ask anyone, and get an answer.
The salsa's on aisle five, next to the dust mops.
Cracked vases and damp hallways–

it's a purely private life. The way
taking it easy is absolutely
full time. The sign language

of windows and doorways, of a man watching a woman
who's watching another man throw down a broom.
Even your faint, familiar voice,

muffled and thirsty,
until its sheer impossibility
moved me over, and I could hear you.

And in this desert of moss, and mountains,
we eat raisins, olives, eggs,
because what is solid

has no opening,
like mourners who have no mouths,
and cannot object, and will remember forever.

Shadow Play

She leaves the motor running.
I would too. I would like to marry her,
that face repeated a million times in this town.
In the exhaust next door a man twists
his wooden leg into an impossible position.
He doesn't even have to say, "I know,
I know, and nobody resents me."
He just grins.

On the vendor's tin scales, daylight
shifts and splinters. Blood on the black brick,
a shopkeeper sweeps glass from his eyelids.
A young man fidgets in a doorway,
cups his hands around a blue
flicker of panic, and leans back
into the shuffling papers and footsteps,
the noise that opens away from him
and is not noise.

Now a cleaning lady stops herself
and looks over her shoulder. And so does
the mailman, a traffic cop, a kid walking his bike.
And the perfect word lodges

deep in the throats of businessmen
talking gibberish, drawing lines around themselves
until obsessed and hailing taxis.
Only our loose clothes

between us, the linen tablecloths, white
as blindness. Only the putter of canal boats,
the vine-covered walls, some cursory
glance that empties our eyes, when they meet,
of options, and won't let go.
A person who might

grow older. People who will dash their dreams.
People who will come back and
live in the aroma of bread, in the sound of
a thousand doves unfolding the plaza.
I would like a glass of ice water.
It's the little thing, when I'm lucky
the world comes to me.

Ralph Angel's poems have appeared in *The American Poetry Review, The Antioch Review, The New Yorker,* and *Poetry.* He is the author of one previous book of poems, *Anxious Latitudes.* His awards include a Fulbright Fellowship, a Pushcart Prize, and *Poetry* magazine's Bess Hokin Prize. He teaches in the writing program at the University of Redlands in California.